Graphic conception:
Sandra Brys

translation: Brian Sullivan of the Alliance
Française of Boston and Cambridge

© Casterman, Tournai 1994
Published by
Charlesbridge Publishing
85 Main Street, Watertown, MA 02172
(617) 926-0329
All rights reserved, including the
right of reproduction in whole or in
part in any form. Printed in Belgium.
10 9 8 7 6 5 4 3 2 1

Library of Congress Cataloging-in-Publication Data
Henno, Robert.
    [Animaux pillards.   English]
    Animal bandits / by Robert Henno; illustrated
by Jean-Marie Winants.
       p.   cm.
    ISBN 0-88106-692-3 (library reinforced)
    ISBN 0-88106-672-9 (trade hardcover)
    1. Animals—Juvenile literature. 2. Predatory
animals—Juvenile literature. 3. Pests—Juvenile
literature. 4. Animals—Food—Juvenile literature.
[1. Predatory animals. 2. Pests. 3. Animals—Food
habits.]   I. Winants, Jean-Marie, ill. II. Title.
QL49.H51513   1994
599' . 053—dc20   93-31750
                                    CIP
                                    AC

ANIMAL BANDITS

by Robert Henno

illustrated by Jean-Marie Winants

Charlesbridge

All animals need food to survive. It is one of the basic, indispensable elements of life. Food is essential for providing the energy that a living creature needs to move about, to escape enemies, to reproduce, and to survive the demands of its particular habitat and social order.

The sources of food

Green plants make their own food by converting the sun's energy. Unlike green plants, animals cannot make food. They must go out and find it. In general, they eat plants or eat other animals. Based on diet, animals can be classified into four groups:

- the herbivores that eat plant life.
- the carnivores that capture living prey.
- the scavengers that eat dead animals.
- the omnivores that eat plants as well as animals.

ANIMALS MUST FIND THEIR FOOD

The bandits

Much of an animal's life is devoted to finding food. The task is even more difficult when an animal needs to provide for its young. For some animals, *stealing* food is a perfectly normal activity.

Natural concentrations of food

A food source may be very large (a colony of nesting birds, for example). Often prey animals live together to protect themselves. Predators that are specialists in robbing nests could wipe out an entire species by preventing any eggs from hatching. When the laws of nature are the rule, however, the numbers of predators and prey are carefully balanced. The growth of a population of predators is always influenced by that of its prey.
Fewer prey animals = less to eat = fewer predator young are born = fewer predators.

The "dining rooms"

The highest concentrations of food are created by humans. For a rat or a mouse, a silo filled with grain or a kitchen filled with food is like Ali Baba's treasure. Given such abundance, the only problem is choosing where to begin eating.

For a fox, a chicken is easier to catch than a crow. Farm enclosures are often poorly built, making it easier for a marten to prey on a domesticated rabbit than to chase after a wild one. Fish breeding ponds are crowded with fish, so why would a heron stand at a river's edge waiting for a fish to swim by? Can we blame these animals for choosing the easy way?

WHO IS AT FAULT?

Are animal bandits bad?

We put human thieves in jail, but animal bandits are a different case. Foxes and stone martens eat a large number of voles, field mice, and even rats. This service more than "pays for" the few eggs or the few hens they steal.

Rats, mice, and migratory locusts are more difficult to defend. Locusts can cause famines in certain regions of the world. Rats and mice, aside from the damages that they cause, can transmit terrible diseases.

Humans, however, often cause the number of these bandits to increase. Certain species have reproduced too much because modern societies give them too much food in the form of public dumps. In addition, people have often wiped out the natural predators of these bandits. Nature can no longer keep the number of animal bandits in check.

THE MAGPIE

A couple of magpies are squawking constantly. At the beginning of the spring, their life is not easy. They face many obstacles as they try to raise a family.

First, the male and female magpies build a nest in one of the big oak trees that border the fields. Worms, slugs, and insects are abundant here, but crows in the area greedily guard this food. The crows attack the magpies and eventually force them to abandon their newly built nest.

The magpies fly off to a small public park and settle in an old chestnut tree. But here, too, they have problems with other birds. This time, screeching bluejays attack them. The magpies try to dodge the angry birds, but they cannot avoid being pecked as they gather materials for their second nest. Soon, the two magpies are forced to relocate once again.

The magpies decide to build their third nest at the top of a fir tree near some houses. Small gardens and well-mowed lawns surround their newest home.

Finally, the female magpie can lay her eggs in peace. She lays six greenish eggs. After 18 days, the babies hatch. The young birds cry out, begging for food. The mother and father search the ground for insects and worms for their hungry nestlings. With long tails bobbing up and down, the magpies pace in all directions on the lawn. They carefully search the flower beds for caterpillars and larvae, but the small amount of food that they carry to the nest does not satisfy their babies.

In desperation, they attack the only source of food available — other birds' nests. One by one, they rob the eggs or young birds from the nests of thrushes, finches, and warblers.

LOCATION	DESCRIPTION	HABITAT	BEHAVIOR

LOCATION

• The magpie is found in temperate North America and almost all of Europe.

DESCRIPTION

• A member of the crow family, the common magpie is easy to identify. It has contrasting black and white feathers and a long, layered tail. In the sunlight, its black feathers reflect shimmering purples, blues and greens.
• The magpie measures 15 to 18 inches in length, half of which is the tail.

HABITAT

• Magpies live in open areas with well-spaced trees, in groves, or in farming regions. They often settle near towns and even in suburbs and city parks.
• They are not found in forests or in mountainous areas.

BEHAVIOR

• The magpie may stay in its territory all year, but it moves to different parts of the territory, especially between January and March. During this time, magpies join together in small groups and chatter non-stop. They pass their time chasing each other and squawking noisily.
• Generally, their chattering is not melodious or song-like. During the nesting season, however, their calls and whistles are more varied.

FOOD

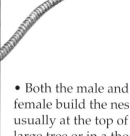

• The magpie usually eats invertebrates, such as insects, larvae, worms, slugs, snails, and spiders. Sometimes it varies its diet with a lizard or a small rodent. It is known to attack sick or injured livestock, and it sometimes feeds on carcasses. The magpie also eats acorns, nuts, berries, cereal grains, and all sorts of fruit.
• Magpies, crows, and jays have a similar diet and compete for food, which often leads to looting of nests.

REPRODUCTION

• Both the male and female build the nest, usually at the top of a large tree or in a thorny shrub. The large nest is a bowl of mud and grass. Sometimes the magpies cover the nest with a dome of twigs.
• The female magpie may lay 6 to 9 eggs between the end of February and mid-June. The eggs are brownish green and spotted with olive brown. The incubation lasts 17 or 18 days.
• Both parents feed the young, who stay in the nest for 22 to 27 days. They stay with their parents until the end of the summer.

THE MAPGPIE AND PEOPLE

• The magpie's contrasting colors, its clumsy appearance on the ground and in flight, and its incessant chattering have attracted the attention of people.
• The magpie has become a symbol of idle chatter and gossip, and even of theft. Although the magpie decorates its nest with shiny objects that it finds, its reputation as a thief is somewhat exaggerated. When songbirds disappear from an area, the magpie is held responsible because it is known to eat songbird eggs.

• For these reasons, some people try to reduce the number of magpies. However, the magpie is often beneficial to agriculture because it eats insects that destroy crops or bother cattle and sheep.

THREATS AND MEASURES OF CONSERVATION

• The magpie sometimes is killed by larger birds of prey or by ground predators, such as cats and foxes.
• When chased away by crows and bluejays, the magpie moves closer and closer to human habitats where its natural food sources are less numerous. Insects, worms, slugs, and spiders cannot live in mowed lawns. They are also eliminated by insecticides.
• To help preserve the songbird populations we could use more natural gardening practices which would allow the magpie's natural food sources to survive.

THE FOX

Peter daydreams in his room. He must hand in an essay tomorrow, and the page in front of him is still completely blank. Suddenly, he hears a noisy commotion from the hen house. Peter rushes over to the window just in time to see a fox run by with a hen in its mouth.

Peter watches the beautiful animal race by. It has a coat of smooth, honey red fur, which is a bit brighter on the sides, and a long bushy tail. It pauses for a moment, making sure it has a solid grasp on its prey. It turns its small triangular head towards the house, then squeezes under the garden fence and disappears in the high grass.

Peter and his mother examine the hen house. The chicken wire is old and full of holes. It must be replaced, but they cannot afford to buy new chicken wire until next week. Something must be done now because this is the second hen that the fox has stolen!

What should they do? Peter and his mother think of possible solutions. They decide not to use a trap or poison because their love of wild animals prevents them from resorting to a deadly solution.

Then Peter thinks of an idea. He says, "How about frightening the fox?"

"How?" Mother replies. "We can't stay in the hen house day and night!"

"What if I set up my radio in the hen house? I could turn on the station that plays continuous music. I bet that would work."

Peter's mother smiles and agrees, but looks unconvinced. Peter moves into action, and soon, the hens hear the "top forty" on the radio.

A few days pass. The fox does not show up. Peter is relieved and proud of himself.

Peter and his mother have a good laugh over the solution. A week later, while they are replacing the chicken wire, Peter tells her about the essay he wrote, "Slyer than a Fox."

LOCATION	DESCRIPTION	HABITAT	BEHAVIOR	FOOD
• The red fox is native to almost all of North America, Europe, and Asia. • The Arctic fox lives on the tundra in Arctic regions. Other kinds of foxes such as the kit fox, grey fox, bat-eared fox, and fennec fox live in South America, North America, and Africa.	• Size: the head and body are 23 to 30 inches long. The tail is 13 to 18 inches long. • Weight: the male may weigh as little as 15 pounds, or as much as 26 pounds. The female is 11 to 13 pounds. • At times its size is overestimated, especially in the winter when its fur is bushy. • Its coat is generally reddish, a sort of russet or red-brown with white underparts. The back of its ears and the fronts of its legs are black or brown. • It has a sharp pointed muzzle and erect ears. The quick movements of its eyes give it an alert, cunning appearance.	• The red fox lives in a variety of environments. It usually lives in forests, plains, or mountains. It also likes undergrowth, rocks, and ruins. It is seen more and more often in suburbs and even in city parks.	• The fox is especially active from sunset until dawn. It can sometimes be observed during the day when it is looking for food for its young. • It generally hunts alone. Its territory varies in size, but it uses its body wastes to mark its territorial boundaries. • Except during the breeding season, the male and female lead solitary lives. • The fox makes hoarse or plaintive barks, short and clear yaps, and growling sounds.	• The fox has a varied diet. Small rodents, particularly voles, are a reliable source of food. Sometimes it will attack a rabbit, hare, pheasant, or even a fawn. This is fairly rare, however, and most often these animals are sick or weak. • Foxes may also eat small birds and their young, fish, lizards, insects, frogs, snails, and earthworms. • Sometimes foxes eat grapes, cherries, blackberries, plums, tender ears of corn, wheat, certain grasses, and wild berries. • They also eat dead animals found by the road. Near cities, foxes have been seen sampling the contents of trash cans. • Foxes do not usually attack chickens or other farm animals unless there are no other sources of food.

REPRODUCTION

- Foxes mate during January or February.
- The baby foxes, called kits, are born 2 months after mating.
- Foxes rarely dig out their own dens. They prefer to take the unoccupied or abandoned burrows of rabbits or badgers.
- The kits are born blind and weigh about 3 1/2 ounces. They are nursed for about 20 days.
- Their weaning is gradual. At first the mother feeds them food she has chewed up or swallowed. At 8 weeks, she brings them live prey. A little later, they follow her and learn how to hunt.
- They become totally independent around September or October.

THE FOX AND PEOPLE

- The fox has so captured our imagination that it is a character in many fables and stories. We often describe this animal with negative human characteristics, such as slyness, deceit, and cunning.

- People regard the fox as a menace because it will raid chicken coops and kill game birds.
- Foxes are very useful to people, however, because they get rid of many small rodents that would otherwise eat crops. In fact, a fox consumes about 6,000 mice each year.

THREATS AND
MEASURES OF CONSERVATION

- In most regions, the fox no longer has natural enemies such as the wolf, lynx, eagle owl, or golden eagle.
- Humans are its main enemy now. In the past, people have hunted, trapped, poisoned, or gassed them in their dens.
- The fox can carry rabies and can transmit this disease to people and livestock. Now, a vaccine against rabies is given to foxes. It is concealed in bait and distributed in regions where the fox lives. The success of these vaccinations is encouraging.

- In many places, foxes are raised, or hunted and trapped for their valuable fur. The most sought after is silver fox, which is black with white tips on the hairs.

THE HERON

John and Maggy rush to finish their breakfast. Two days ago, Grandmother gave them ten goldfish, and they can't wait to go look at them. With the last mouthfuls of cereal just swallowed, they run to the far end of the garden. Sitting on the edge of the pond, they toss small pieces of bread onto the water. Soon, the fish come to the surface to nibble at the bread. 1,2,3,4 . . . 5. Each time they count, they get the same number. Five of their fish have disappeared! But there are no dead fish floating on the surface. Could Fluffy, the neighbors' cat, be responsible? The children decide that is unlikely because the water is deep enough for the fish to avoid the cat.

They decide to hide in the small shed at the far end of the garden. They wait for over an hour, but nothing happens. All of a sudden, they hear a noise above them.

"There's something on the roof," whispers John. Maggy places her finger over her lips, motioning for him to be quiet. Less than a minute later, a shadow moves across the lawn, and a large bird lands. It is a heron. Alert and wary, it turns its head slowly from left to right.

Reassured by the calm and quiet, the bird shakes itself, then begins to carefully preen its feathers. Its long neck undulates in all directions.

It stops preening when it catches sight of movement near the water's surface. Like a robot, it approaches the pond with slow, jerky steps. It moves into the water and stops. Nothing happens. The bird holds itself as still as a statue. The minutes slowly pass. The children hear their own heartbeat.

Suddenly, the neck of the bird snaps forward like a spring, and the heron plunges its head beneath the water. Then it flaps its wings to regain its balance as it pulls its head out of the water. At the end of its long beak, a goldfish wriggles. The heron throws the fish into the air, catches it, and swallows it head first.

"My fish!" shouts Maggy. Frightened, the heron flies away. Its "crah, crah" resounds in the sky.

LOCATION	DESCRIPTION	HABITAT	BEHAVIOR

LOCATION

• The common gray heron is found in almost all of Europe and in temperate regions of Asia and Africa.
• A closely related species is the great blue heron of North America, the West Indies, and the Galapagos Islands. The great white heron, the little blue heron, and the green heron are other types found in the United States.

DESCRIPTION

• Gray is the main color of the common heron's plumage. It has a long white neck, which folds into an S shape during flight.
• The feathers at the tip of the wings are black. A black line also decorates the front of its neck. The adult has a black band above each eye that extends to the crest that covers its head.
• It has a slender beak and very long legs.
• Its height is 36 inches. Its wing span is 5 feet.

HABITAT

• The heron lives in wet places such as marshes, ponds, lakes, rivers, and estuaries as well as in nearby wooded areas. It is often seen near sea shores and in fields that border streams or channels. Its long, widespread toes allow it to walk on muddy, slippery banks.

BEHAVIOR

• The heron may live alone or in a group. It usually nests in a colony of two or more species of birds. It is especially active during the day, but also hunts and flies at dusk.
• Its flight is slow and heavy. With its head drawn back and its legs trailing behind, it flaps its wings as if in slow motion.

• It perches on a tree branch with wings lightly spread apart to bask in the sun.
• When it is disturbed, it flies off, letting out a loud "crah, crah" sound. In nesting areas, it makes a guttural cackling: "kakakaka."
• It can stand on one leg without moving for so long that it looks like a statue.

FOOD

- The heron's diet is varied. It eats fish, frogs, tadpoles, crabs, beetles, worms, voles, and even small snakes. It usually stands in shallow water near tall grasses to hunt.
- The heron does not stab or pierce its prey. Instead, it uses its bill to grab the prey and quickly throw it into the air. The heron skillfully catches and swallows it, head first. Prey that is too large or that can put up a long fight, such as an eel, cannot always be swallowed easily. The bird brings this type of prey to the shore, where it kills it before eating it.

REPRODUCTION

- The common heron sometimes nests in isolation, but may also nest in a colony of a hundred or more pairs. It builds its nest in trees, bushes, or reeds. The heron often uses the same nest year after year, repairing it each spring.
- The egg laying season begins at the end of February or the beginning of March. The female lays from 2 to 6 light green-blue eggs. Both parents incubate the eggs for 24 to 28 days and raise their young together. The babies stay in the nest until their feathers are grown. After about twenty days, they perch on the edge of the nest and on neighboring branches. They cannot fly or leave until 50 to 55 days after they hatch.

THE HERON AND PEOPLE

- In the past, people who caught fish or raised fish on special farms believed that herons threatened their livelihood. They killed so many herons during the 1950's that people began to fear the species would become extinct. Studies during that time revealed that the heron's effect on fish breeding populations was very small. Today, this bird is protected in many countries, and its numbers are increasing again.

THREATS AND MEASURES OF CONSERVATION

- The heron can be a nuisance to commercial fish breeders. Herons will visit commercial fish farms because they can easily catch their fill of fish. Some fish breeders ignore the laws that protect the herons. However, there are many ways to scare away the herons and to protect the fish. A blank-shooting gun makes enough noise to frighten away herons. Placing nets along the banks of ponds keeps herons out of the areas where they can catch fish.

THE MARTEN

Greatly excited, Amy, Adeline, and Allan hurry home after running errands for their mother. They rush in and tell her that they saw "several wild beasts" running on the top of an old house.

"They were pretty big," says Adeline, "like a cat, but longer. We didn't see them very well because it was starting to get dark."

"I was afraid," adds Amy. "When they saw us, they stopped. They turned their heads and looked right at us before they ran to the other side of the roof."

Their mother looks skeptical. She knows that her children have active imaginations and are always inventing stories. "That's very interesting," she tells them. "Come sit down at the table. Dinner is ready. You can tell your father about it while we eat."

Allan, the youngest, greets their father with a smile and a hug. Then they all sit down, and the children tell him about what they saw. Allan says, "I saw them, too!

The beasts were going to eat. They had white napkins tied around their necks!" Everyone laughs, and the older children agree that the animals did have white fur like a bib.

Father listens attentively to the children's story and praises Allan for his good observation. "It's a family of stone martens," he explains. "They're very pretty. Their coat is brown-beige, and they have white patches on their necks and chests that do look like bibs. You don't need to be afraid of them. They won't hurt you. Stone martens love to play games and do somersaults. If you like, we'll try to go see them again one night soon."

"By the way, did you know that the high pitched cries of the stone martens and the noises of their games at night made people think their houses were haunted? That's why people around here used to tell ghost stories."

LOCATION	DESCRIPTION	HABITAT	BEHAVIOR

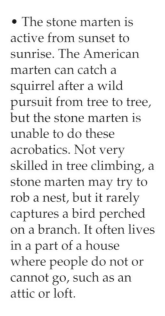

LOCATION

- The stone marten is found all over continental Europe and in central Asia.
- There are many other species of martens, for example, the American marten, the pine marten, the Japanese marten, and the yellow throated marten.

DESCRIPTION

- Like most of the members of the Mustelidae family, which includes the badger, otter, skunk, ferret, and other weasel-like mammals, the stone marten has a long, slender body, short legs, and a wedge-shaped muzzle.
- The slightly curved back is flexible and arches when it moves so that martens are agile and graceful animals.
- Its fur can vary from brown to grayish beige with a white patch from the top of its neck to the top of its forelegs.
- From its head to its body it measures 16 to 20 inches. Its tail is 9 to 11 inches long. The height to its shoulders is 5 inches.
- The male weighs 4 to 5 1/2 pounds. The female weighs 2 1/2 to 3 pounds.

HABITAT

- The stone marten likes human habitats. It can be found in attics, barns, hay lofts, wood piles, ruins, and old walls. In contrast to the American marten, which is clearly a forest dweller, the stone marten goes only as far as the edge of the woods and only when the woods are near a farm or house where it lives.

BEHAVIOR

- The stone marten is active from sunset to sunrise. The American marten can catch a squirrel after a wild pursuit from tree to tree, but the stone marten is unable to do these acrobatics. Not very skilled in tree climbing, a stone marten may try to rob a nest, but it rarely captures a bird perched on a branch. It often lives in a part of a house where people do not or cannot go, such as an attic or loft.
- The stone marten is quite noisy, especially at mating time and when playing. The noise often scares people who live in a house that martens have invaded.
- The stone marten makes a great variety of noises including piercing cries, yaps, whistles, and growls.

FOOD

• The stone marten is sometimes classified as a carnivorous animal. In reality, it is omnivorous (eats both plants and animals). It also adapts its diet to what is available each season. Its most common foods are small rodents, such as mice, voles, and rats. It also will eat eggs and steal birds from their nests. Sometimes it eats insects and earthworms.

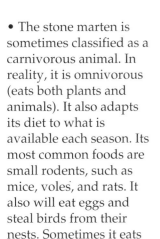

• During the summer and fall, it eats many fruits such as apples, pears, and cherries.
• It may also raid hen houses and pigeon houses to kill and eat the fowl.

REPRODUCTION

• Although mating takes place in the summer, the pups are not born until April or May.
• The pups are born blind and with no fur. There are 2 to 4 in a litter. When they are weaned after 6 to 7 weeks, their mother brings food to them. At the age of 3 months, they are capable of catching prey themselves.

THE STONE MARTEN AND PEOPLE

• The principal occupation of the stone marten is catching rodents such as the brown rat. These rats are so fierce that even cats avoid attacking them.

• Although the stone marten is very useful, it has a bad reputation, mainly for the following reasons:
- it scares people with its cries and the noise that it makes during certain times of the year in attics and lofts;
- it sometimes raids chicken coops and other domestic bird enclosures.

ROLE

• The stone marten is a very beautiful animal and interesting to observe. It poses no threat or danger to people and fills an important and necessary role as a predator against rodents.
• Wire fences can protect chickens and other domestic breeding areas where martens might be bothersome.
• When martens try to live between the rafters of a house, their noises can be very unpleasant. The best solution is to seal off their entry. This can be done when the stone martens are not "at home" and do not have a litter of babies living inside the house.

THE MOUSE

The mouse slowly circles the trap and sniffs it. The piece of cheese on the small wooden board looks appetizing, but the mouse is wary because just a few days ago, it saw one of its sisters get caught and die in a spring trap of the same type.

Although the mouse is a master in the art of stealing bait, it is careful. It draws back a little, darts forward, hits the trap, and leaps back immediately. Nothing happens. The mouse tries again at a different angle. This time the trap moves half an inch but does not release. The mouse carefully inspects the trap and then tries again.

Snap! The trap brushes past the tip of its nose as the mouse leaps back. What a close call!

Without losing any time, the mouse begins to nibble at the bait. It eats and then cleans itself before heading on its way.

The mouse passes a dish of poisoned seeds but does not stop. It has been a long time since it has sniffed at this dangerous bait. It

hears a scampering noise behind it and pauses. It turns its head and sees a younger mouse heading toward the seeds. The younger mouse looks starved. It is probably an orphan without any experience. The older mouse makes the other one understand that these seeds, despite their tempting appearance, should not be eaten.

A few minutes later, they both creep under the door of the pantry where the people keep their food. They hungrily eye the shelves of boxes and bags containing a variety of delicious food.

But how can they get up there? The step stool that was there yesterday is now gone. Jumping up to the first shelf is impossible. The mice begin to climb the bottles placed against the wall.

A last jump and they reach a hanging braid of garlic. Like acrobats, they climb the garlic. Each one loses its balance and almost falls, but they are finally close to the food.

Here is a jar of peanut butter, but after sniffing it the two mice know they cannot get any of the wonderful food inside. They inspect each jar, tin, and package by sniffing it. Finally, they find a large plastic bag of rice. The picture of a smiling man looks down on them as they gnaw a hole through the plastic and hungrily begin to devour the rice, piece by piece.

While they are filling their stomachs, they are still watchful and wary of every sound. It is always best for them to be careful because they can smell that a cat has been in this house. It's not easy to be a mouse!

LOCATION	DESCRIPTION	HABITAT	BEHAVIOR

LOCATION

• Originally, the gray mouse lived on the Asian steppes, in northern Africa, and in the Mediterranean area.
• Today, it is found all over the world, mainly because of its remarkable ability to adapt and reproduce.

DESCRIPTION

• The mouse weighs about 1/2 ounce (10 to 15 grams).
• The length of its body is 3 to 4 inches.
• The length of its sparsely-haired tail varies greatly. Most often, the tail is the same length or is only slightly shorter than its body.
• The typical house mouse is charcoal gray while outdoor mice are fawn brown. The fur of both is slightly paler on the underside. Mice have moderately large ears and eyes, and a pointed muzzle.

HABITAT

• The gray mouse usually lives near people. Even in prehistoric times it shared their shelters. This is why it is often wrongfully called a "domestic mouse." (A domestic animal is one that is raised by people who have some use for it.) It is also called a "house mouse" because colonies of them live in barns, attics, basements, or other human-made buildings.

BEHAVIOR

• Mice live in family groups. Members of the same group recognize each other by their smell.
• The social structure of a mouse colony is quite unformed until the population reaches a point of overcrowding. Then a social hierarchy forms, led by one dominant male who is generally stronger than the others. Because he will not permit the other males to mate with the females, this leads to a natural end to the overpopulation problem.
• Mice are nocturnal animals and generally stay hidden during the day.

FOOD

- Mice are basically seed and grain eaters, but readily adapt to a wide variety of other foods.
- In human environments, the mouse is an omnivorous animal, eating all organic material. Although it especially appreciates the food of people, it also will eat other materials such as paper and leather.
- Mice that live in houses do not store food. They gather their food on a daily basis. In contrast, mice that live outdoors build up large supplies of food in preparation for winter.

REPRODUCTION

- Mice that have protection from the cold and plenty of food can reproduce all year long. If not, the season of reproduction lasts from spring until fall.
- The female makes a nest out of anything that she may find such as straw, hay, or pieces of cloth.
- She gives birth 20 days after mating. She can have from 4 to 10 young, but the average litter is 5 or 6.
- The young are capable of finding their own food at the age of 15 days. They can reproduce at the age of one and a half to two months. A female can have as many as 10 or more litters a year, but usually has 5.

THE MOUSE AND PEOPLE

- Mice cause much damage to the houses in which they live. They may gnaw holes in walls, floors, furniture, upholstery, and clothing. Their teeth are sharp enough to tear some of the toughest materials.
- They often steal and contaminate stored food.
- Like the rat, the mouse can carry illnesses that are dangerous to humans.
- For all of these reasons, people often try to exterminate mice. Natural predators, such as cats and owls, can effectively control most mouse problems.

THE WHITE MOUSE

- The white mouse is an albino form of the gray mouse. The Egyptians bred it several thousand years ago. Today it is widely used in laboratories by scientists who do medical research.

THE BROWN RAT

Night has fallen, and all is calm in the henhouse. Perched on their roosts with their heads tucked under their wings, the hens sleep soundly.

Beneath the floor of the hen house, however, there is a commotion. While everyone else sleeps, the brown rats are busy. Three playful young rats bump into the other rats in the pack, who are grooming themselves. The three jostle each other, nibble at one another, roll on top of each other, and begin a wild chase. The mother rat shows her annoyance, and soon they calm down. She closely watches over her newborn babies, resting in a nest made of hay and a piece of burlap.

Her three older offspring prepare to leave the shelter for the first time. They will explore the surroundings and learn how to find their own food. Their uncle will be their guide. Among the members of the family, he is the oldest and the most experienced. He knows how to detect and avoid traps and poisoned bait left by the farmer.

When the three young rats leave with their uncle, they follow him single-file toward the hen house. One after the other, they squeeze through a crack in its floor.

The last one is distracted by everything it sees, and lags behind. It stops in front of a hen sleeping on the lowest level of the perch. Standing on its hind legs, the rat sniffs at the toes of the fowl. This looks edible! Without hesitation, it nibbles at the toes. Awakened with a start, the hen cries out and flies up. The rest of the hens awaken and cackle anxiously.

Panicked, the young troublemaker hurries to rejoin the others. They rush through an open window and run back into the basement of the farmer's house.

As the farmer runs outside with his rifle in his hand, the noises in the hen house fade and die away. Confused, he returns to his bed.

The rats continue to explore. They soon find the smell of food.

Unfortunately for the rats, however, the farmer's wife has had enough of their stealing and has locked everything in metal boxes. The hungry young rats gnaw at the end of an empty cereal box.

Then their leader discovers an opened bottle of olive oil. Very quickly he knocks off the cap and jumps to a higher shelf. He lowers his tail into the bottle below and then takes it out and lets the delicious liquid drip into the open mouths of the hungry young rats. What a feast!

LOCATION	DESCRIPTION	HABITAT	BEHAVIOR	FOOD

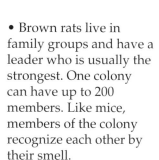

LOCATION

• The brown rat originally came from Asia. By stowing away on ships, it spread throughout all of Europe by the 18th century. It came to America with the early settlers. Today it is found all over the world.
• It is called by many names: wharf rat, Norway rat, sewer rat, and even house rat.

DESCRIPTION

• The length of the head and body is 9 to 11 inches.
• The length of the tail varies but is almost as long as the body.
• It weighs 9 to 21 ounces.
• Its fur is a coarse brown-gray, and its stomach is a grayish white color.
• The hairs of its tail are fairly short, so that it looks naked.
• The brown rat differs from the black rat in the color of its fur, the size of its ears, which are smaller, and by its less pointed, more rounded muzzle.

HABITAT

• The brown rat is found more often in cities than in the country. Most brown rats live close to humans: in basements, markets, slaughterhouses, stables, and hen houses.
• They often burrow holes beneath the floor or in the walls of dwellings. Brown rats also like damp environments such as sewers. Black rats, on the other hand, prefer high spaces like attics and rooftops.

BEHAVIOR

• Brown rats live in family groups and have a leader who is usually the strongest. One colony can have up to 200 members. Like mice, members of the colony recognize each other by their smell.
• Each member of a colony has a certain social status which allows it to intimidate other rats or requires it to submit. The brown rat does not have an aggressive temperament and rarely fights with other brown rats. The elders educate the young.
• The brown rat is especially active from dusk until dawn.
• When it feels threatened by a predator, it faces its enemy and defends its life. Its bites are deep and painful. Cats and dogs often fear rats and prefer to retreat rather than confront one.

FOOD

• The brown rat gnaws constantly. It gnaws on almost anything: walls, lead pipes, plaster, furniture, insulation, books, rugs, and so on. Like all members of the rodent family, its front teeth never stop growing. Since its teeth grow 5 inches a year, it must constantly grind them down by gnawing.
• The rat is omnivorous. It eats seeds, table scraps, carcasses, fabrics, leather, paper, and so on. It may even attack small livestock. It can kill a chick or even a full grown chicken. It especially likes eggs.
• Generally, the rat does not store food, so it must search for food each day.

REPRODUCTION

• The brown rat can reproduce all year but usually mates in the spring and autumn.

• The female gives birth 3 weeks after mating.

• The young are born blind and with no fur. They open their eyes after 5 to 6 days.

• The young are weaned and leave the nest at the age of 6 weeks.

• The rate of reproduction is very rapid:

- a female can have 4 to 5 litters per year.

- a litter can consist of 5 to 15 young.

- the young are capable of reproducing at the age of 2 to 3 months. This explains why in large cities there can be more brown rats than inhabitants. However, the size of family groups depends on the amount of food available. When they are threatened by lack of food, brown rats reproduce less often.

ENEMIES

• Owls and martens are the rat's predators. In Asia and Africa, its predator is the mongoose. The mongoose has been brought to North and South America to help control the rat population, but the mongoose will often eat birds and other animals instead of rats.

water rat

THE BROWN RAT AND HUMANS

• The brown rat is a true pest for humans. It consumes a great deal of our food and contaminates even more. It causes enormous damage gnawing away at everything it finds in its path. It attacks pipes and metal barriers. It can even cause buildings to collapse. Nearly 50% of fires due to short circuits are caused by rats gnawing through plastic wire coatings.

• Babies, young children, and invalids have been bitten by rats.

• The brown rat carries many diseases. The most well known is the Bubonic plague, which caused the death of millions of people hundreds of years ago. The brown rat can also transmit typhus, leptospirosis, and rabies. The fight against brown rats is not easy because they are often smart enough to avoid traps and poison.

black rat

THREATS

• The brown rat's survival is well assured. Rats occupy almost every type of habitat.

brown rat

THE MIGRATORY LOCUST

The farmers are looking forward to a good harvest. Although this region of Africa has suffered from droughts in the past, this year they will harvest large crops of corn, millet, and sorghum. The children, playing happily, do not notice the sky darkening as if a curtain were being drawn between the sun and the ground. A group of women, who are doing their laundry in the stream, suddenly shout, "The locusts, the locusts are coming!"

Boubé and his friends are terrified. They remember the stories told by the village elders about the invasions of the locusts.

"Hurry! Go help your parents! Hurry!" shouts the leader of the village.

The insects surround Boubé's body as he runs home. The humming from their wings is deafening. He tries to swat them away.

When Boubé arrives at his family's fields, his parents hand him a cloth soaked in water. Like a windmill, he whirls it around against the swarms of locusts. In less than a minute, Boubé kills over a hundred, but no matter how many he destroys, it makes little difference. Millions and millions of locusts swarm around the village, devouring the crops.

Boubé keeps swinging the cloth until his arms hurt. Finally, the cloud of locusts goes away.

Boubé sinks to the ground wearily. Everything growing in the area has been eaten. Boubé searches the small bit of land his father gave him to grow his own vegetables. There is nothing left in his garden. He looks at the cloud of locusts in the distance as tears roll down his cheeks.

LOCATION	DESCRIPTION	HABITAT	BEHAVIOR

LOCATION

• The African migratory locust is found in Africa and in southwest Asia. Its areas of reproduction are mainly the following countries of Africa and Asia: Sudan, Chad, Niger, Mali, Mauritania, India, Yemen, and Saudi Arabia.

• The Rocky Mountain locust has caused great destruction, sweeping over the western part of the United States and parts of Canada.

DESCRIPTION

• Its length is 2 1/2 to 3 inches. The female is longer than the male.
• It weighs less than an ounce (2 to 4 grams).
• Young locusts are spotted with black. Adult locusts are yellow spotted with black.
• The locust has two large compound eyes and a pair of short antennas on the top of its head.
• It has 6 legs. The two back legs are much larger for jumping.
• The larvae resemble adult insects, but are much smaller and only have stumps instead of wings.

foot

HABITAT

• Migratory locusts are found in semi-arid regions. Rain plays an important role in their development. The eggs need moist soil in order to develop, and the larvae need vegetation and water to thrive.
• These conditions exist only during certain times of the year, for a short period of time, and in very limited areas. To find these places and conditions, the locusts are capable of undertaking great migrations.

BEHAVIOR

• Locusts exist in two stages: a solitary stage and a swarming stage. When they are crowded together, they change their behavior and may also change their color.
• In their solitary stage, they are not noticed because they are not noisy.
• Under certain weather conditions scattered solitary locusts may come together in favorable laying sites. There, they reproduce and multiply so quickly there may be as many as 3 generations in ten months.
• Hoppers, or flightless, immature locusts, may form bands on the ground. Billions of adult locusts form swarms which can obscure the sky. Migrating swarms are capable of traveling over a thousand miles between breeding grounds.

FOOD

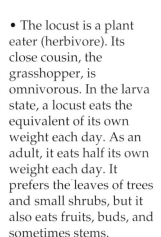

• The locust is a plant eater (herbivore). Its close cousin, the grasshopper, is omnivorous. In the larva state, a locust eats the equivalent of its own weight each day. As an adult, it eats half its own weight each day. It prefers the leaves of trees and small shrubs, but it also eats fruits, buds, and sometimes stems.

REPRODUCTION

• The migratory locust can mate all year long. To attract a female, the male vibrates its wings. These vibrations do not produce any noise but release a hormonal "smell" that attracts the female. After mating, the female digs a deep hole in the ground and lays about a hundred eggs.
• The larvae hatch in about 10 days. To become an adult insect, a larva goes through 5 stages. In 20 days, it is mature and able to reproduce.

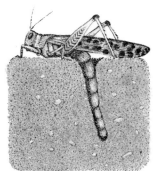

THE MIGRATORY LOCUST AND PEOPLE

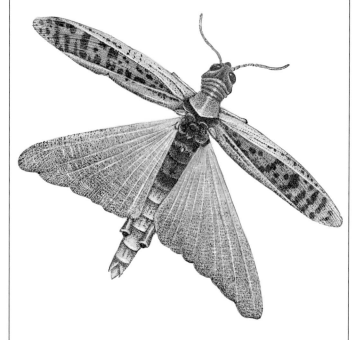

• In the Bible and the Koran, the invasions of migratory locusts are interpreted as a divine punishment. Locusts can devastate entire regions and cause catastrophic famines, especially in regions impoverished by years of drought. The very rain that allows cultivation to start again can also cause thousands of locusts to hatch.

THE FIGHT AGAINST THE LOCUSTS

• Planes can spray insecticides onto the swarms to kill a large number of locusts. However, the chemicals have adverse effects on birds and livestock and the people who live in the treated zones.
• Prevention is the best way to fight the locust invasions. Many organizations work to locate the areas where adult locusts gather and mate so that they can prevent the locusts' reproduction. Unfortunately, political problems such as wars hinder the ability of these organizations to act effectively.

THE STARLING

Two starlings search carefully in the fields for insects. They are in luck! They find a deposit of cranefly larvae and peck it out of its hiding place. With beaks full, they fly back to their nest in a nearby orchard. They place the food in the wide-open beaks of their six babies and leave again to search for more food.

The babies soon find the way out of their nest in a hollowed out tree trunk. Curious and hungry, the hatchlings peck away at everything they discover. The bravest walk out toward their parents so that they are fed first.

The young are soon able to fly. They perch on branches in the orchard and look around curiously. The father stabs into a well-ripened cherry, and soon the nearest of his young imitates him. A second and then a third family of starlings join them. They all enjoy the cherries. Instead of completely eating a few fruits, they peck a little on all the ones that seem appetizing.

The starlings cause serious damage to the orchard. The farmer has been trying to get rid of the birds for several years with little success. Now they are so used to the loud noise of his gun that it does not frighten them away.

One thing does cause panic in the flock. Like a bolt of lightning, a sparrow hawk suddenly appears in the sky and swoops down to grab a starling. With its prey held tightly in its claws, the sparrow hawk flies off. The starlings turn around in the sky in a tight band. Fearful that their enemy will return, they soon leave to find another orchard feast.

LOCATION	DESCRIPTION	HABITAT	BEHAVIOR

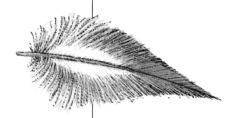

LOCATION	DESCRIPTION	HABITAT	BEHAVIOR
• The starling is native to most of Europe and western and central Asia. • Brought to North America in 1890, huge flocks of starlings are now a common sight.	• Its length is 8 ¹/₄ inches. • Its weight is 3 ounces. • The baby starling is a dull brown color. The adults have a yellow beak and black feathers with a glossy shine of brown, purple, green, and blue. Its feathers are tipped with pale brownish-white which forms triangular specks or tiny v's. • It is stocky, with a very short tail, a longer and more pointed beak than a blackbird, and shorter legs. On the ground, it does not hop, but trots rapidly, shaking its head back and forth.	• Originally, the starling was a bird of the forest. • Today it can be observed everywhere — in cities, towns, woods, rocky zones, and farms. Large groups of starlings are common, especially in developed regions.	• After mating and bringing up their young, starlings form flocks, sometimes with thousands of members. When they fly, they form a gigantic cloud. During the day, they often spread out for feeding, but in the evening, the groups reunite to spend the night together in a grove of trees. • The starling's song is varied. It is most often a combination of whistles, clucks, clinks, and many other noises. It can also imitate the calls and cries of other birds and even mechanical sounds.

FOOD

- Insects form the basis of the starling's diet. It may eat harmful larvae and land snails in plowed fields, grasslands, or lawns.
- It also likes fruits, such as cherries, apples, pears, grapes, and strawberries.
- It can also eat crops such as corn and grain.

REPRODUCTION

- The starling searches for nest holes in trees. It often takes nests hollowed out by woodpeckers. The gradual disappearance of old trees has not caused the same problems for the starling as it has for other species because any hollow, natural or artificial, is a good place to raise its young. It can build its nest in the holes of walls, beneath the eaves of homes, or in nesting boxes.
- The nest is made of leaves, straw, and grass.
- The eggs are a very pale blue and sometimes have small red spots. The female lays 5 to 8 eggs, which hatch in 12 or 13 days.
- Both parents feed the young until they leave the nest after 22 to 25 days.

THE STARLING AND PEOPLE

- Starlings are a nuisance in towns and cities. Their resting areas, often the tops of buildings and window ledges, are very noisy and foul smelling if there are a large number of starlings in the group. Their cries and the incessant squawking of the young begging for food can be annoying. People try to drive them away but have little success.

- When a flock of starlings swoops down on an orchard or a vineyard, it can completely wipe out a harvest in a few hours.
- For these reasons, humans often try to kill the starlings with traps, snares, and poison.

THREAT

- Although a flock of starlings may eat vast quantities of insects, it may also devour an entire field of strawberries or eat all the grapes in a vineyard in fifteen minutes!
- Loud noises may frighten starlings away for awhile, but are not effective for long.
- At some airports, birds of prey are used to keep starlings away from runways. Serious accidents can occur when the air intake on a jet engine becomes blocked by a flock of thousands of starlings.

THE HERRING GULL

The herring gull hovers in the sky. Gliding silently, it searches for a colony of terns and their hatchlings. The gull's own young were born a little over a week ago, and they are hungry.

The gull circles around and lands on a rock. From this perch, it looks out at its surroundings. Its keen eyes spot a chick at the edge of the terns' territory.

With a flap of its wings, the gull leaves its perch and moves toward its prey. The flock of terns flies up to meet the challenger, cawing sharply. They are aware of the danger to their chicks. Their only advantage in the battle is that there are so many terns to peck on the gull's head.

The terns' pointed beaks are dangerous weapons, but the gull has its size and strength to its advantage. It dodges its attackers and continues its approach. The diving attacks of the terns continue and become more precise. Harassed on all sides, the gull gives up. The victorious terns chase the gull for a few moments and then return to their nests.

Frustrated, the gull stops for a minute to smooth its feathers. Then it flies to a nearby cliff in search of different prey. The gull knows that many puffins come to nest in the burrows on the grassy summit.

The gull spots a puffin that has returned from fishing. Small fish droop from the sides of its multicolored beak. It stands a few feet away from the gull and watches it uneasily. It must pass by the gull to get back to the burrow where its young are waiting. The puffin slowly walks forward. Suddenly, the gull attacks.

Frightened, the puffin tries to fly away, but the gull quickly catches it, seizing it by its feathers and tail. Unbalanced, the puffin makes a turn in the air, opens its beak, and lets the fish fall. The gull abandons the puffin, steals the fish, and returns to its waiting chicks.

LOCATION	DESCRIPTION	HABITAT	BEHAVIOR

LOCATION

• The herring gull is found in North America, Europe, Asia, and North Africa.

DESCRIPTION

• The herring gull measures 21 $^1/_2$ to 23 $^1/_2$ inches long.
• Its wing span is 4 feet, 8 inches to 5 feet, 3 inches.
• The wings and the back are gray, the tip of the wings are black, and the rest of the body is white.
• The beak is yellow with a red spot on the lower part.
• The feet are webbed and yellow.
• The young gulls have dark brown feathers spotted with light brown. Color varies with age, however, and does not become permanent until the gull is 3 or 4 years old.

HABITAT

• The gull was at one time found only near estuaries.
• Today, it can be observed near lakes, rivers, and on land, even far from the ocean.

BEHAVIOR

• The herring gull may live in groups or alone, but it often flies in flocks.
• It may follow fishing boats to collect scraps or to catch small fish that escape from the nets.
• It also follows field-plowing tractors to eat worms or other invertebrates brought to the surface.
• It often raids domestic garbage dumps for abundant and easy food.
• When the gull finds food, it may bring some to the members of its flock or communicate the location to them.
• The gull also eats mussels and other shellfish. It carries a mussel or clam into the air and drops it onto a rock to break open the shell.
• It raids colonies of terns and other seabirds, taking their eggs and their chicks.
• The gull harasses puffins, pelicans, and other fish-catching birds until they drop the food that was supposed to be for their young.
• It occasionally attacks adult birds.

FOOD

• The herring gull is omnivorous, which means it eats everything it can find — fish, shrimp, crabs, small mammals, birds, seeds, and garbage.

REPRODUCTION

• Herring gulls generally nest in colonies.
• They prefer to nest on cliffs, small islands, sand dunes, or near colonies of other seabirds. The gull does very little nest building. The nest might be a shallow hole in the sand with some seaweed or twigs loosely strewn about.
• The female lays 2 to 3 eggs.
• The male and female take turns incubating the eggs for about 30 days, but the female does most of this work. The young are raised by both parents.
• The young are capable of flying at the age of 6 to 7 weeks.
• Herring gulls return regularly to the same nesting place with the same mate.

THE GULL AND PEOPLE

• The success of gulls has often led to the reduction of the population of other species. To allow populations of other birds to survive in certain areas, the gulls' eggs are injected with a chemical so they will not hatch. If these eggs are simply taken away, the gull will lay more eggs.
• Flocks of several hundreds gulls can create health problems because of the large quantity of excrement they produce. This can pollute ponds and harm the native plant life that provides a habitat for both land and marine animal life.

THREATS

• Despite the many measures taken to limit its overpopulation, the herring gull is still multiplying rapidly.